THE FINAL PIECE OF THE PUZZLE

BY

JEAN L. EMBRY

Dear Deb,
Deanne and Vern — Whenever there's a smile in church — you're a part of it. My life has really been a happy one and you've been a part of it. There's joy all around it, too! You're a part of it. God Bless.
luv ya, Jean

TRAFFORD
PUBLISHING

© Copyright 2006 Jean L. Embry.
All rights reserved. No part of this publication may be reproduced, stored in a retrieval system, or transmitted, in any form or by any means, electronic, mechanical, photocopying, recording, or otherwise, without the written prior permission of the author.

Note for Librarians: A cataloguing record for this book is available from Library and Archives Canada at www.collectionscanada.ca/amicus/index-e.html
ISBN 1-4120-7413-4

Printed in Victoria, BC, Canada. Printed on paper with minimum 30% recycled fibre. Trafford's print shop runs on "green energy" from solar, wind and other environmentally-friendly power sources.

Offices in Canada, USA, Ireland and UK

This book was published *on-demand* in cooperation with Trafford Publishing. On-demand publishing is a unique process and service of making a book available for retail sale to the public taking advantage of on-demand manufacturing and Internet marketing. On-demand publishing includes promotions, retail sales, manufacturing, order fulfilment, accounting and collecting royalties on behalf of the author.

Book sales for North America and international:
Trafford Publishing, 6E–2333 Government St.,
Victoria, BC V8T 4P4 CANADA
phone 250 383 6864 (toll-free 1 888 232 4444)
fax 250 383 6804; email to orders@trafford.com
Book sales in Europe:
Trafford Publishing (UK) Limited, 9 Park End Street, 2nd Floor
Oxford, UK OXI IHH UNITED KINGDOM
phone 44 (0)1865 722 113 (local rate 0845 230 9701)
facsimile 44 (0)1865 722 868; info.uk@trafford.com
Order online at:
trafford.com/05-2308

10 9 8 7 6 5 4 3 2

THIS BOOK IS DEDICATED TO:

ALL OF MY FAMILY AND FRIENDS!

Thanks to my Mom and Dad who taught me: the joy of living life everyday; to realize that "tomorrow is not promised to you" (a hard thing for me to learn – being the recovering procrastinator that I am – smile); they taught me that all humans deserve a free life, much love, and always the pursuit of happiness- and that THIS includes me. I have tried to live up to this!!

My friends have been my' Family' down through the years and this book is dedicated to them: To Judith Krause – who has been there for me and remains my steadfast friend, editing and correcting the errors that I have made, staying up until the wee hours of the morning on many occasions, helping me make the deadline – and always having confidence in me. To L.C. Myles – without him I never could have made this computer do what I want it to do. I can always count on his unswerving patience with me and his never ending encouragement for me to accomplish this feat. To Jackie McGrady – always here when I need her and always in my corner with the greatest of faith in me. To Evelyn Lowe – who knew all the time that I could do it and said so, and said hurry up!

To Shirley Hunter – always as close as the phone and 'checking in' and checking me out. To Elease Holmes: Gently nudging me to get with it, listening and appreciating my stories. To Catherine Dade – Everyday – How's the book coming?? When is the book coming?? To Frances Wimberly, who always had time for me, and Christine Miller-Betts who encouraged me to write a book. To Len Brown – gone but certainly not forgotten. I can still hear his complimentary comments, laughter and enjoyment of my work.
To the many other friends who hung in there with me all of the way. Finally to – My beloved Grace Ball, my wonderful neighbor, who did not live to see or read my book- heard many excerpts from it, but I know she knows that I finally did it! Thank you again and again!!
And yes, this is just the beginning! Just the FIRST PIECE OF THE PUZZLE.

CONTENTS

I.
WITH GOD'S BLESSINGS

1.	God's Colors	11
2.	My hand in God's	14
3.	If There is Ever a Time	15
4.	God Is Real!	16
5.	Good Morning God	21
6.	Trust in the Lord	25
7.	Dawning of the World	27
8.	That Special Christmas Tree	29
9.	I Am Unique!	31
10.	God is!!!	35
11.	Our Heavenly Father	41

II.
MEMORIES

1.	My Father's Hands	45
2.	The Wisest of All	47
3.	I'm Going To Find Myself	50
4.	Clouds and Two Kids	52
5.	Remember Mom	54
6.	Until We Meet Again (My Retirement)	58
7.	(Papa) Please	60
8.	A Journey With The Moon	62
9.	His Voice	66
10.	Our Friend Mel	69

III.
P.S. I LOVE YOU

1.	The Quiet of My Living Room	75
2.	My Friend	77
3.	Happy Valentine's Day	78
4.	From Friend to Friend	80
5.	Did I Really Care Enough?	84
6.	Dawning	87
7.	P.S. I Love You	88

IV.
THOUGHTS and DREAMS

1.	This Really Happened	93
2.	My Dreams – #1, #2 and #3	96
3.	Superstitions	103
4.	Please Say Yes	107
5.	Our Palms	109
6.	Believe Me It's Nice To Be Home	111

V.
GOOD GRIEF! LIFE IS GREAT!!

1.	This Bush is Mine!	119
2.	Velma's Place	121
3.	At the Polls	128
4.	Toenail Poisoning!	130
5.	The Survivor	137
6.	The Mysterious Old Gentleman	139
7.	You Beautiful Rose	144
8.	Because I'm Getting Old	146

9.	Teacher, Teacher	148
10.	Please, Pass It On!	149
11.	Le Generale	151
12.	It's Your Birthday	154
13.	I Should Have Known	156
14.	I Should Have Known –Continued	159
15.	How Do We Do It?	163
16.	HELP!!	164

I.

With God's Blessings

GOD'S COLORS!

As I sit here and muse at the edge of the woods
I marvel at the many gifts God has given me.
With my back against a wise old oak –
　this panoramic view
Commands my deepest humility.

There are grassy rolling greens
that are so vivid you can smell them.
There are canary yellows and maple reds
　of brightness almost impossible
　to describe.

Their radiance and color richness
　make you want to touch them
And your senses say they're very much alive.

There are shrouded mountains
　and butterflies of purple
That shout out echoes of their sheer delights.

The many shades of blue
　that hold the massive sky up
Tug with the orange streaks – a spiritual sight.

There's a black – that's decidedly
　deep with emotion
You'll find it in caves and on caterpillars
It envelopes you like a mist from the ocean
And sends chills down your spine –
　like some thrillers.

There are lavender forget-me-nots
  and teal blue ocean waves
That will fool you as they sparkle and play.
There are browns of the muskrat
  and tans of the deer
A mauve clump of thistle
  that springs back every year.

The red of the cardinal and the rose of the rose
Are painted like words that are written in prose.
The gray fog coming in
  and the diamond stars coming out
Wield a wand of silver webbing –
  a silver lining all about.

The crimson leaves of the walnut trees
  and the flaxen coat of the fawn
Are demonstrations that the artist is undaunted.
The chirping of the birds
  startling the quietness of the hour
Keeps me from feeling that my haven is haunted.

The chartreuse of the salamander
  and the maroon of the hills
Compete from afar with the white-golden sands
And the velvety magenta of the apples on the trees
Are part of the landscaper's plans.

The artist that did this,
The One who imagined the world in its
Grandiose colors
Dipped onto his rainbow-filled palette,
  and made the whole thing
From a void that resembles no other.

God threw colors around and
He found all the crevices
To paint and – He used finger-painting.
He swirled, danced and wove,
  and playfully strove
To put all of these colors together.

So brilliant the hues –
  make such beautiful views
And they change all the time –
   like the weather.

An artist I would be, but never
  like you see this wonderful world –
  with such luster ——.

So, I sit here and paint,
  'neath this loving oak tree
And I ask –'Oh, Great Maker –
  please shower on me – a tad of your talent';
And you will agree
that even the rabbits and squirrels watch to see
  the brilliance of brush and stroke –
  copying the need
To capture this moment – forever.

SO, HATS OFF TO A GOD
WHO KNOWS JUST WHAT HE WANTS
AND PAINTS FOR US —
THESE MAGNIFICENT COLORS!!

MY HAND IN GOD'S

Each morning when I wake I say,
"I place my hand in God's today."
With faith and trust that by my side
He'll walk with me, my steps to guide.

He leads me with the tenderest care,
When paths are dark, and I despair.
No need for me to understand
If I but hold fast to His hand.

My hand in His; no surer way
To walk in safety through each day.
By His great bounty I am fed,
Warmed by His love, and comforted.

When at day's end I seek my rest
And realize how very much I'm blessed,
My thanks pour out to Him, and then -
I place my hand in God's again

My uncle ___Louis Sullivan_____
       has gone to rest
He placed his hand in God's, he's blessed..

IF THERE'S EVER A TIME

If there's ever a time when we should
Count our blessings – THIS I S IT!!

If there's ever a time when we should
Forget our petty differences, look at
Our friends with love and warmth,
And see each other in each other's eyes
THIS IS IT!!

If there's ever a time when we should
Banish from our brains, have washed
In the rains, thoughts and feelings of
NEGATIVE strains that we let enter
Our domain – THIS IS IT!!

Let's put our arms around our friends,
Wondering whether this is the end of
Our journey – Maybe – THIS – IS — IT!!

If there's ever a time when we should
Enjoy our blessings – THIS IS IT!!

GOD IS REAL!!!

I know there is a God
There are so many reasons–
And He is here for us, no matter when.

He's our calendar-maker –
In charge of the seasons
And He is – Always –
Not just now and then.

He's in the high ocean waves
   that break at the shore
And in the heart of your puppy dog
   as she stretches on the floor.

He's in the beauty of huge boulders
   that stand end-on-end,
And in the canyons of splendor
   whose bright colors blend.

He's in the form of a young child
   with his thumb in his mouth,
And in the honking of geese
   in formation, going south.

He's in the giggle of a baby
   happy all by herself,
And in the chuckle of your spouse
   once he's fixed that old shelf.

He's in your thoughts of a dear friend
   you've not written for a while
   and she calls you with those same
   thoughts – from away across the miles.

He's the echo in the mountains –
   When you holler – helloo – hello –
He's the wind in your face –
   And the rain falling slow.

He's a pasture of buttercups –
And that old man walking to town;
He's in the laughter of children
   just running around.

He's with kittens, and teenagers;
A musical sound – from a harmonica,
   a violin, or a bass drum you pound,
   from a piano, a French horn,
   a steel drum and fife –
   a waterfall, bells tinkling —
   sounds you've heard all your life.

He's in my impatient loved one,
   Just waiting to go.
He's in quiet surroundings –
   after the first fallen snow.

He's with Mom in her kitchen
   just baking some bread.
And with Pop as he quietly
   snores in his bed.

He gives me protection
   throughout sadness and gloom,

And watches over me at night
   while sleeping in my room.

He's with robins and swallows,
   canaries and flamingoes,
He's on the high seas and rivers
   and wherever the wind blows.

He's with the bride and the groom,
   The slow rocking of old ones.
He comes when you call –
   And you just have to call once.

He's in the gnarled hands
   Of grandma who served all her life,
He's in grandpa's stooped shoulders,
   From labor and strife.

He's in the sobbing of someone
   whose heart has been broken.
He's thunder and lightening
You know God has spoken!

He's in the twinkling stars,
   the universe with many planets;
He's in the depths of a mineshaft
   And on great mountains of granite.

He's in the heart of the elephant,
   the platypus and porpoise,
   the whale and the wildebeest
   the lion and the tortoise.

He's in the runners and sprinters
   and dancers and walkers, –
   singers and swingers
   and whistlers and talkers.

He's in the stockrooms and courtrooms,
   And boardrooms — HE'S HERE!!

He's our security blanket that says:
   "Have No Fear!"

He makes the seeds in the ground
   grow to all kinds of things –
He puts the tears in our eyes –
And the eagle on wings.

He's that song in my heart –
   I keep humming all day
   because He knows it helps keep
   my troubles away.

My God made each human,
   and holds us in his palm,
Our every need is satisfied
He keeps us from harm.

But, we must realize the truth –
His Omnipotent power rules.

He never gives us more
   than we can bear –
He gives us the tools to handle life,
   whatever the collection,
     just pray for His protection.

He knows we're poor mortals needing
   guidance and direction.

So, just listen, He'll find you —
Say a quiet prayer in your heart
And God will stay with you
Yes, He'll never part!!

Yes, Oh Yes. MY GOD IS – REAL!!

Good Morning God:

Good Morning God, How are you today?
Thank you for listening to all that I say.
Thank you for understanding me

when I pray.
Good Morning God!

Thank you for sunshine,
  and rain and for snow,
For wind and the bird's song
  and for evening's glow;
For pine straw and squirrels
  and grass that is green
For blue skies with white clouds,
  seashores that are clean..

Thank you for the full moon
  that makes us act strange;
For horses and buffalos
  and cows on the range.

Thank you for mountains and valleys,
　　oceans and streams
With trout and with salmon and
　　crappies and breams..

Thank you for elephants
　and tigers and bears
For all things that live and breathe –
　we know that You care..

Thank you for good friends
　　that always seem there
And for loved ones and families,
I ask in my prayer.

Thanks for the mean ones
　　and grumpies and frowners
And stingy ones, pious ones,
　　spoiled ones and pouters;.

For happy ones, crying ones,
　busy ones and buyers
For rich ones and poor ones
　and stealers and liars.

For dreamers, and schemers,
　　and astronomical folks,
For wagers, backstagers
　　and those who tell jokes.

For little ones and big ones,
  the old and the young
And all those in between
who like to have fun!

For hoarders and detainers,
  explainers and complainers,
For huggers and muggers,
for all these I pray.

For poets and writers,
  the stoic and the fighters
For the givers and the takers,
for lovers and wave-makers

For the mourners and the grievers
For the jealous and believers,
For the know-it-alls
  and the show-it-alls;.
The gullibles and the deceivers,
This morning I pray.

Thank you for loving us,
  the good and the bad,
For sending us someone
  with a smile when we're sad.

For partnership, companionship
and warmth when we're lonely
Thank you for reminding us that
You and You only –
   Love us because we are <u>Yours</u>!!

Good morning God! Have a great day!

TRUST IN THE LORD

Proverbs 3: 5,23.

I trust in the Lord with all my heart
For each morning, each sunset,
Each miracle derived;

For each failure, refusal,
Each falter, each try,
For each comfort, acceptance,
Each hello, and goodbye.

I love the Lord completely
And know that I do
Appreciate the wonderment
Of each gray sky or blue.

I marvel at each moment,
At each time that I'm true
To my commitment, my love
And my faith in Him, too.

I trust Him, for each river of sorrow,
For each ocean of joy –
Yes, He is the toy maker,
And I am the toy.

I thank Him for His understanding
For each laugh and each hug,
And for each time I'm crushed
He gives my heartstrings a tug,

Saying "You'll be alright,
Keep your hand in mine".
I am rich with His blessings
Rich all the time.

I thank Him for each friendship,
Each dream, tear and sigh,
Each day that I live is filled with
Greatness, and that is why –

I trust in the Lord, with all of my heart,
And I'll walk my way confidently,
　My hand in God's hand,
And I will not stumble nor
From Him ever part.

    AMEN

DAWNING OF THE WORLD

I've decided to walk on the beach
  once more
And sink my shoes in the sand.
This is my last morning at the shore,
The weekend has really been grand.

What a wonderful ecstatic feeling
To be alone with my thoughts
  in the dark.
I realize this rapture occurs
  every time that I
Stroll on the beach or take a walk
  in the park.

The moon casts a strange glow
  on the sand dunes and gullies
And empty beach houses
  stand stark and grim
But my Creator and I walk hand in hand
With my faith and my trust
  explicitly in Him.

Ah, riding on the highest waves,
Over the edge of the world surfs the sun
Producing a magnificently gleaming glow
Toward which the little straight-legged
   sandpipers run.

The surf is quite happy saying,
  "watch me, come on in and catch me,
I'm primed for a show."

As I continued to walk
The wetness abounded
And the breathtaking scenery surrounded me
In time and tune with the sonorous sound
Of the Ocean.

I WONDER IF THE WORLD WERE THIS WAY
           AT ITS DAWNING.

THAT SPECIAL CHRISTMAS TREE

Have you ever sat down quietly
   to watch your Christmas tree?
And marveled at the twinkling lights
   that seem so bright and free –
And felt the warmth of the different balls,
   some red, blue and some gold
And thought the Christmas story is
   the one that won't grow old?

Have you watched the sparkling
   Christmas lights, blinking in syncopation?
And mused at how the kids and grown-ups –
   wait in anticipation
For the enigmatic Santa who never
   seems to appear
But leaves his droppings here and there,
   scurrying behind his tiny reindeer?

Somewhere in the background you hear
   Christmas carolers singing
And listen to the church bells giving out
   sonorous ding-dong dinging.
But then, you think of loved ones
   and the people that you know
And how each is represented on the tree,
   with their very special glow.

All of us, like each little light,
   on this Christmas tree,
Shine, twinkle, some on and off,
   and some shine continuously.

If only we'd take note of ourselves
   and see our incandescence
I'm sure we'd glow with great degree,
   we'd stop and count our blessings.

Let's say, this little Tannenbaum –
   represents our world
And Christ is at the very top,
   keeping each branch unfurled.
Let's say a prayer for the universe
   and all that we might treasure
And thank the Lord, again and again,
   for His blessings without measure.

MERRY CHRISTMAS
     AND HAPPY NEW YEAR!!

I AM UNIQUE—
(WE ARE ALL UNIQUE)

You are you — and I am me!!
In all the world there is no one
  exactly like you or me.

There are persons who have parts
  and perhaps looks like mine-
But, looking at the big picture,
  no one adds up exactly like me.

Therefore, everything
  that comes out of me
  is authentically MINE
    Because God alone,
    chose it for me!

God owns and knows
  everything about me.
He knows all of my triumphs
  and successes,
all of my failures and mistakes;
the good me,
    the bad me
        and the in between me.

However, I can control almost
  everything about me –
    the choice is mine.

I can control my body,
   my mind, my thoughts and ideas;
      my eyes including
   all of the images I behold;
      my feelings whatever they may be –
love, anger, joy, frustration,
   disappointment, excitement, warmth;

My mouth
   and all of the words that come out of it-
polite, sweet or rough, correct or incorrect.

My voice – cold or warm, loud or soft;
      and all of my actions—
(including my sense of humor)–
   whether they are to others or to myself.

I can become lazy
   and put everything on automatic
and thereby lose control.
I can say it wasn't my fault.
   I can find excuses – or,
I can take responsibility for my actions.

By being able to control myself,
   I can become intimately acquainted
      with God.
I can love and be friendly with me,
   in all my parts.
Therefore, God makes it possible
   for me to work together in my
      best interests.

There are aspects about myself
   that puzzle me,
     and other aspects
that I don't even know,
   but as long as I am friendly
     and loving with myself,
I can courageously and hopefully
   look for the solutions of the
       PUZZLE
that I am, and ways to find out more
   about my 'puzzling' self,
     putting the
PIECES OF THE PUZZLE
     together,
  as directed by God.

How I look and sound,
   whatever I say and do,
and whatever I think and feel,
   at a given moment,
represents where I am,
 at this particular time.

Later, when I review me,
   some parts of me
may turn out to be unfitting.
I can discard that which is imperfect
and keep that which proved
   fitting, and invent something
      NEW
to take the place of that
   which I discarded.

By the Grace of God,
I have the tools to survive!! –

To be close to others, to be productive,
to never feel alone, and to make sense
and order out of the world of people,
places and things, that surround me.
The locus of control is in 'ME'.

    I AM ME!!

I AM A VERY SPECIAL PUZZLE,
AND THANKS BE TO GOD,
    I AM OKAY!!

GOD MADE ME, AND OWNS ME!
AND GOD DOESN'T MAKE MISTAKES!

GOD IS!!!

GOD IS LIFE!!

God gives life to everything-
All creatures, great and small –
And makes us humankind responsible
For all His world – yes ALL!

From ants to eagles, lions and seals
He even taught us how
To manage, handle, breed or bring forth
All things, with life endowed.
To weed and seed and clean and feed,
   To plant and plow and water;
To care and share and save from wear
   All living things, we ought to.

But, we are shiftless, mean at times,
   And sometimes selfish, too.
We know to do good is His command;
   This means me and you.
We know we don't do all we should
   To keep our planet healthy.
We're much too busy getting ahead,
   Making progress and getting wealthy.

Yet, there are those of us who care
   A lot about His creatures.
So, we ask God to give us strength
   And wisdom, as His teachers.
There are some folks who can still learn
   About their God given responsibilities –

And with His help and guidance,
   We can strengthen their abilities.

Our Heavenly Father, keep us focused
   On how to do Your will –
And we thank You, Lord,
   for all Your blessings —
Our lives, and hearts, please Lord, we pray,
   With love, You'll always fill.

GOD IS LAUGHTER — # Hee-Hee — HA HA — OOOH!

(GOD WITH HIS LAUGHTER PLAYS A GREAT ROLE!!)
This is how WE do it: Picture This —

Hitting our thighs
  Crying and wiping our eyes
    Stomping the floor
      Holding our sides!!

Choking and gasping
  Holding and grasping
    Screaming and yelling
      Ha- Ha! –ing and bellowing!

Splitting and jerking
  Howling and smirking
    Rolling and waving
      Ranting and raving!

Chuckling and stifle-ing
  Rubbing and Rifling.
    Tee-hee-ing and Ooh-wee-ing!
      Slapping and Dapping!

Tittering and guffawing
  "There ought to be a law –ing"!
    Oh-ump-ing and chrrump-ing
With mouth open or closed.
  Falling on the floor
or bouncing on our toes!

Giggling and wiggling
  Jumping and wriggling!
    Snickering and working
      ourselves into a lather —
Sides hurting, we're blurting — stop it!
  Can't stop heaving, even if we'd rather!

Like a brook babbling,
  We chortle and hoop!
    Like a bunch of kids
      Sitting on the front stoop!!

Laughter is great – especially
  AT OURSELVES –
     And when it's permitted –
     At somebody else!

All over the world laughter is the same
  It's a language of its own –
    Needs no answer – no name!

Laughter is contagious
Epidemically outrageous,
Wonderful to be around
Regardless of culture or lineage!
The laughter of God is a beautiful sound
And we are made in His image!

God with His good humor,
    plays a great role —
And He shows us that LAUGHTER
  is good for the soul!!

GOD IS — LOVE

   GOD IS GOOD ALL THE TIME!!

God is Love:
   A love that's all encompassing
That one cannot explain—
As rain and snow come down from Heaven
   And do not return again –

To water our earth,
   fill our lakes and rivers,
And freshen mountains and plains –
 God is good!!

God showers us with sunshine
To give each day a smile
He shares His moonshine with us, too,
To keep us tipsy for a while.

God loves us, we're His little children
And to our Father we must go –
No matter how we feel
   we can do it alone –
We find that that is not so.

God 's love demands that
   we love one another
As well as we do ourselves
And He rewards us three and four fold,
And seven times seven times seven
Our cups forever overfill.

God is with us and watches over us
Wherever we may be
He's promised to never leave us
His riches are all free!

God made us individually
With creativity and talents.
He expects us to use our gifts for Him
To keep His world well-balanced!

Our Heavenly Father has great patience
    with us
He has given us so many reasons to be
Thankful, joyful, spiritual and true
Reasons for happiness
   and sorrowful times, too.

He lends us our loved ones
Takes them back in His time.
Be grateful we had them,
They're His, they're 'not mine'.

The paths our loved ones traveled
To make our lives better
Are blessings God gave us,
Like the seasons and the weather.

Stop – for a moment
Look around you and start
 counting your many blessings!
His love never parts!

GOD IS GOOD ALL THE TIME!!!

OUR HEAVENLY FATHER

Our Heavenly Father, Creator of Heaven and
    Earth,
Blessed art Thou on the glorious throne of
    Thy Kingdom.
You have showered me with your bountiful
    Blessings and I thank You.

Bless this little book, and please make it
    Available to those who need a little joy,
    A happy chuckle, a smidgin of a smile,
    A sense of peace, and a moment to
    Step away from our frenzied world

I thank You, O' Great God, for the privilege of
    Sharing my talents. Forgive me my sins,
    And help me to humbly walk in Your
    Ways, and delight in Your will,
    To the glory of Your name. AMEN

II.

Memories

MY FATHER'S HANDS

Were large with tapered fingers,
  so open and giving.
They held my hands, turned screwdrivers,
  And tops,
And helped him earn a living.

They buckled and buttoned,
  tied shoelaces and wires;
Watered the flowers and changed the tires;
Braided hair, used trimmers, blew noses,
  shoveled snow;
Papered the walls, checked fuses,
  went shopping and
  Chose my clothes.

Showed deep feelings, and action,
  fidgeted when waiting;
Restrained me, but never alarmed me,
  steadied me when skating.

His sensitive hands were
  expressive and fan-like;
Played the piano, fixed chairs,
  and taught me to ride a bike.
Put back chicks in their nests,
  pointed out butterflies;
Dressed up like Santa Claus,
but was no big surprise –Ha!

Straightened my coat,
  brushed lint from my shoulders;

Clapped at my performances
  making me feel bolder;
Told me to learn extraordinary charm
  from my mother-
Told me she had 'it' — really like no other.

At a big dinner,
  his slow turkey-carving,
  seemed meticulous and ridiculous –
  when I was starving.

His hands on his chin
  with that big boyish grin;
He waved goodbye
  whenever he was leaving.
Yet, when he got back,
  he whistled through the crack
  in his fingers for me,
  catching the ball, dodging and weaving.

He never left me without telling me
  he loved me,
  and, that I should continue to worship
the Great Man above me.

As long as I live,
  I'll remember his grand motions,
Helping me understand,
  the meaning of love and devotion.

He made my life wonderful,
  with all that he touched,
With his hands.

THE WISEST OF ALL

Aeschylus the Greek dramatist said,
  "It is always the season
  for the old to learn".
There is always a reason
  for huggin' and squeezin',
    and letting the warm fires burn.

It is always a surprise
  for the young to be wise
  and the wisdom just drips like a faucet
Yet, I can attest to their wisdom at best,
  that babies are the smartest of all sets.

So, what do they do?
They just look at you,
  and you wipe and you rock
  and sing songs.

You change and you play
  and you always stay
  within their sight or
  you have really done wrong.

You burp and you pat,
  sling them onto your back,
  and find your hand moist
  from the diaper.

So, you hurry up and change
   whatever is in your range
   to retrieve that great smile
   like a windshield wiper.

They'll coo and they'll kick,
   suck their big toe like a stick and
Keep you busy from sunup to sundown.

They'll look in your eyes
   and seem quite surprised
   that you are just a little bit rundown.

The milk must be just right,
   the food must be just right,
   the water and juice all the same.

The only time you get
   to sit down, wipe sweat
   is when all of the baby's needs are met
   and your spouse
      is now calling your name.

The old have to learn
   that grandparents can turn
   a mellow baby into a monster.

A cough – pick him up,

  a blast, pick him up,

  a cry to stretch his lungs –

PICK HIM UP!!!

They can croon, tunes they've got,
  or chuckle and rock to their hearts content –
  but the baby cares not –
"get off the pot and give me what ever I want,"
just like a gangster.

It's always the season
  for the old to learn!

DON'T BET ON IT!!!!!.

I'M GOING TO FIND MYSELF

Saturday Morning about 9:00

You say:
Pick my shoes up, make my bed
Eat my oatmeal, do not snack!

You check my email, check my videos
I am thirteen
And I'm gonna pack!!

Don't like my hair, don't like my music
Don't like my pants, my this and that
Don't like the way I eat my hotdog
You don't even like my cat!.

Johnnie said he ran away last week
They had to bribe him
To come back!

That ain't my style
Now, I'm leaving
I ain't never coming back.

Get up early, do my homework
Eat the same old meal at night
Vegetables, casseroles, ham and turkey
What's wrong with
  a Big Mac to do it right.

Did I tell you that I'm leaving?
This is the very end!
You won't find me at the basketball court!
Your old dumb rules-you don't ever bend!
And I thought you were a good sport.

Don't wait up for me tonight —
Mow the lawn and wash the car
I am grown-- I know what's right!
And I'm traveling – very far!

Can't take my cell phone, or my videos?
Wish I could drive, can't take my bike?
You are mean right to the end.
That's okay, you're gonna miss me;
I'll just hang out with my friends!

Saturday Afternoon about 3:00 pm

Hi Mom!! Did you miss me?
I sure am hungry!! What's for dinner?

CLOUDS – AND TWO KIDS

It's so nice out here in the park
We gotta get home – way before dark.

See those pretty clouds, Jackie?
Way up high and fluffy?

This one looks like a beautiful castle –
That one looks just like my dog Tuffie!
This one, right over our heads,
  looks just like our house.

Yeah! See that one over there?
 It looks like a cat - chasing a mouse.

Oooh, I like that one,

It looks just like a clown –
  and that one looks like a bell
  Upside down –

And that one looks like a big bird
  Flying around. Wow!

Jeannie: I don't really like
  that dark one –
Way over there – it looks so sad.
Do you think clouds get whippings
when they've been acting really bad?

No, girl, what's wrong with you?
We're the only ones that get a
   switching!
Gee, I know those clouds are glad!

I like this cloud – I like that one –
   It's so soft and pretty.
I got some dirt on my Jeans,
And look, your shoes are gritty.
Ants are crawling –
Uh,oh – I hear somebody's calling
   -------Oooo –oooo.

 Jackie, don't you hear
   your Momma calling you?

I'll race you home!!

REMEMBER MOM

For those of you with mothers
  who are living today –
I'm sure you have sweet memories
  and maybe what I say –
May be a reminder of the things
  in the past
So, thank God for your mother,
  may her presence always last.

And, for those of you
  whose loving mothers are no longer here –
Perhaps you, too,
  remember those things I hold so dear.

Remember how, as little tots,
  we wanted to do – more –
And she would give us little chores
  and send us to the store?

Remember we'd go shopping
  and she'd buy our favorite fruit;
And how we'd get into the car
  and give the horn a toot?

Remember, how she'd look so hurt
  when we did something wrong?
And she'd make us eat Popeye's spinach –
  to make us big and strong?

Remember how the days were short
  and nights seemed oh, so, long
'cause we planned to get up early
  to do something with our mom?

Remember how she'd comb our hair,
   and it would really hurt
And how we'd get a spanking,
   when all clean, we played in dirt?

Remember how she'd wipe our noses,
   how we hated that
And when we had to go to church
   she made us wear –'that hat'?

Remember how she'd kiss us –
   once we jumped into our beds
And tell us bedtime stories –
   and we'd go to sleep instead?

Remember on those cold days –
   she would make our favorite chowder?
And how, as kids, we loved her make-up,
   lipstick, rouge and powder?

Remember almost breaking our necks
   when we put on her high heels
And thinking we were fooling her,
   when we felt like making deals;

And in the winter she would
   make us eat that lumpy oatmeal?
And take to school that great big lunch
   that didn't even seem real?

And once we had a puppy –
   who kept nipping at her heels
And she said it would have to go
   –'cause it just 'wets and squeals'–?

Once we came home,
  late from school
  and mom was worried sick –
She said if we did it again,
  she'd beat us with a stick!

Remember the night she was so tired,
  she fell asleep at the table
And we cleaned up just everything
  for mom –'cause we were able.

Remember when we chalked the sidewalk –
  and made a huge hopscotch
And mom came out and played the game –
  but the rain made it a splotch.

Remember when we had a cold,
  she'd give us castor oil?
And heaven knows the stuff she'd use
  if we ever had a boil.

And remember on one steamy night –
  she left us shed our nightgowns
And we laughed at each other,
  screamed and giggled –
  we acted like such clowns.

Remember my first date and Pop said
  "No lingering on the front",
And mom said, "Why not, you sure did
  and performed all kinds of stunts."

Once we got engaged she said
  a very important thing –
That 'Faith and love and heartache
  are all wrapped up in that ring!"

Remember at my wedding
  we were walking down the aisle
And mom sat there so beautiful –
  And forced a tearful smile –
And afterwards she hugged me tight
  and said, "You're still my baby",
But, right now, chin-up-happy child –
  Show them you are a lady!"

The years have passed, she's gone away
  but she hasn't really left me.
She's in my thoughts most everyday
And I remember what she taught me.

Her spirit lingers everywhere –
  and in the glow of evening
She's that shining star – so close up there
  With love, she's not bereaving.

She's helping someone else in heaven
  in her own quiet way –
And I look forward to the time
  When she and I will say – "Remember!"

UNTIL WE MEET AGAIN

    (My Retirement)

There comes a time in everyone's life
When great changes come about.
You see I'm closing a door behind me
And now I'm stepping out.

The job I've been performing
Has lasted over the years
So you can see why leaving it
Will definitely bring tears.

New vistas, new horizons
Are all opening up for me,
But a little tinge of sadness
Is perched up in my tree.

I'm leaving an old way of life
And starting out anew;
But the sadness comes
   when I think I might
Be parting from you and you!

We never know what life will hold
And that's good – it's really a test.
'Cause some of us would think the worst
But some would dream the best!!

So far, life's been a roller coaster
And I've enjoyed it all.
I feel I've been so truly blessed
You bet!! I'm standing tall!

I'm keeping a stiff upper lip
And I'll just say a prayer
That all of us will have good health
And happiness to share!

Until we meet again!! Until we meet again!!!

PAPA PLEASE!

Papa, teach me how to dance
Show me what to do.
How to do the 'lectric slide
And the boo-ga-loo.
Mama says it's so much fun
When she dances with you.

Papa, teach me how to skate
To do the figure eight!!
Hold my hand, don't let me fall;
And I can learn to brake.

Papa, teach me how to ride my bike
You gave it to me for Christmas
And hold the seat, so I won't fall
Then, I can pedal it this much.

My feet just hardly touch the pedals
  I wish that I were tall.
Be careful, Papa, I'm so little.
I'm zigzagging for a sprawl! Ouch!

Papa, teach me how to swim
The butterfly stroke is great!
Mama says I'm not old enough
But, gee, I'm almost eight.

One day, Papa, you'll teach me how
To drive a pretty car;
I'll pump the gas, wipe the windows–
I won't drive it very far —
Unless Mama says it's okay.
    Papa, PLEASE!!

A JOURNEY WITH THE MOON

What is more wonderful than
　lying in bed
With my hands behind my head
Watching the moon through my
　window
And feeling the moonbeams – it sheds.

This luminous, long-lasting light
Shines through the trees,
And dribbles soft incandescence
On branches and leaves.

The moon's not a man or a woman
It's really a celestial being
Suspended in space – for the
　whole human race
To plant by, to walk on,
　or simply for seeing.

It does more than just drift
In the sky all alone,
And more than reign over us
Like a king on a throne.

It lights the pathway of a traveler
Walking alone
Who is threading his footsteps
　quickly
On his way home.

It glows through the window
On the face of a young mother
While rocking her baby to sleep
"Shhh – little brother".

It shines into a gully
Where three deer are standing,
And the glistening antlers
Of the buck – are commanding.

This moonlight is free
And works with abandon
It lights up a mountain,
  a river, a landing,
An owl and a muskrat,
  on or under a tree.
It bathes a hapless and a homeless one,
A prisoner trying to flee.

It's not really fussy,
  it shines with the sun –
Once in a while –
And believe me,
It's hard to explain to a child.

Our moon may have a visitor,
The North Star, in flight -
And perhaps a constellation
To party with tonight.

It brings songs to the dogs
  and the wolves
Late at night –
Who are drawn to its magnificence
And crystal beams bright.

Making love in the moonlight
Is a comet strip – you soar –
As you go step-stoning on stars –
You and your lover roar –
  out of space –
To universal places –
Like Venus and Mars!!

When God in His wisdom
Created the moon
He knew it would safeguard us
From darkness and gloom.

His moon knows its humans
And takes care of them duly
But, there are those
  on a full moon
Whose actions are unruly.

Yet, this celestial being
Envelopes them in happiness
With a special type of beauty
No other can convey –
  by its godliness.

You see, there is nothing
  more wonderful
Than lying in bed
With the soft tranquil moonbeams
All glowing 'round our heads –

And this wonderful gift
God loaned us for a while
We should notice – be thankful
And return its stellar smile!

HIS VOICE

Low, husky, masculine
Then, the question, "What's up?"
The answer is not too much
   to his liking,
So the range and timbre run amuck!

"If you want to work for nothing
   Then, you don't need me!
   Your worth is far greater
   Than you're given credit
    I can't seem to make you see!
This is just another scam
A pipe dream --a ruse.

You've worked hard to achieve
   your status
You've paid your dues!!

I know how wonderful
   your knowledge about the world is
   and now, you're gonna be used!
I get so angry when you do this!"
And his voice became high-pitched.

"Don't you remember the last time
   you helped someone
They became a disappearing witch?"

Of course, there was only silence
  on my end (of the line).
Listening to his thought-provoking
  screams
I said, "I know I need to make
  more money – to raise my economics-
And I'm open to almost all themes –
  not dreams."

W e l l, with a pronounced groan –
  and a very fast-paced
"Do what you want, but
  don't expect me to help" –

I'm glad I couldn't see his face.

Don't want to lose him as my agent!
My mind is running all over the place.

He said, "I'll talk to you later,
  Ciao!" Bang! Went the phone!

My spirit was spiraling up,
  but now it's on the ground.
What can I do? My head's spinning 'round.

I feel all alone, sometimes I hate the phone!

My heart felt displaced –
from the speed that it raced
My tongue felt distaste –
my eyelashes tear-laced.
I prayed for "His" grace.

There is little more to say,
So, I'm leaving it this way! THE END.

OUR FRIEND MEL

There is a nice fella named Mel,
  who has lots of stories to tell.
        He suffers a fate
        That at an uncanny rate
He can eat a spread that is unbelievable!

We work with him every day,
  and he's fun, and he has a nice way.
  His usual lunch is popcorn –
  with Snickers' Bars hidden away.

So, this is how the story went;
  we took Mel to lunch during Lent
        'Cause he was leaving
        And we were grieving
The loss of this man Providence sent.

The restaurant was of local renown
However, not dressy, no tux and no gown.
        We enjoyed the entrance
        Went in and sat down
And we were quite happy
  just looking around.

Our arrival was less than noteworthy;
  the service was nice but quite slow.
        Mel's appetite was strong
        He had waited too long
And he was impatient and wanted to go!

We tried to calm his agitate,
  and so he decided to wait.
        Eating pickles and bread
        Drinking iced tea instead
As we talked – and it was getting late.

He'd made no Lent resolutions,
  and he said a gourmet he was not.
        He said that he ate
        What was put on his plate
And he'd be happy when he got what he got.

Finally, the waitress served
  him a gargantuan plate
Which was piled as high as a mountain.
The whole plate was covered
  spilling over the sides to the placemat
        Like a musical fountain.

The waitress smiled when she served him,
Gently placing the plate on the table.
        He gazed with desire
        He was on fire
But we didn't think he was able.

He didn't say much –
  when in front of him
  sat brazenly this breathtaking crate
        So we marveled and jeered
        Argued and cheered
That he'd never eat in 300 years,
  all of the food on his plate!

He picked up his fork with a great flair
And waved it in the air with a great flourish.
Like an M-16 he began to attack
Everything on his plate that would nourish!

Well, Mel ate and he ate
  and he cleaned off his plate
Sat back with his arms
  folded in front of him.
    And we gawked and we stared –
    not to say that he cared
(As we looked at his plate) –
  but we'd never, no never
            Make fun of him!!   HA!

We asked dear ole Mel,
  how he felt –???
   Once he returned to the office
     He unbuttoned his shirt
     Then, he loosened his belt
And we could tell that he was no novice.

He exclaimed, with a sigh,
  that he felt pretty good
  Even though he had et and et
  all of that food.

So o o, the meat of the story,
  and the proof of the test –
Don't eat fast like Mel
  who needed 'Gas-X',
'Cause he ate and he ate
  and he cleaned off his plate;

The size of the meal was incredible.
Needless to say, Mel ate it all –
Everything on the plate that was edible.

The moral of the story is a good one
Kudos to our colleague and worker
  'Cause when it comes to debate
    Mel takes the cake
He's our gastronomical guru
  and NO SHIRKER!!

Well, we'll miss dear ole Melvin,
  we wish he could stay
And we'll remember our ole friend
  at lunchtime – everyday!!

    GOOD LUCK, MEL!!

III.

P.S. I Love You

THE QUIET OF MY LIVING ROOM

Lovely memories come to me
While I sit in the quiet of my living room.
Remembering the thrill of our very first date
When our love began to bloom.

Our first communication
   was an argument about
Some arbitrary rules, some nonsense –
   right or wrong –
And it seemed so foolish as we talked
   and shouted for our point,
That we were laughing –
   until crying at ourselves- before long.

The telephone calls, the chance
   but not so chancy meetings.
That seemed just to happen at times –
The palpitating heart,
   the daydreaming, the songs
And even the poetry,
   the sentences that rhyme.

The constant looking forward
   toward seeing you each day
The matter of humdrum,
   invasive work – the paying job –
That seemed to get in the way.

I know for me, my heart hasn't changed
And your voice still lights my fire
Your touch still creates warmth in me,
   and radiates your desire.

The quiet jazz is playing
   one of our favorite tunes
Bringing back lovely memories,
   while we sit close together
In our quiet living room.

My Friend

Companionship for perfect years
Along life's busy road
Was ours to share forever
But now I carry the load.

Death stops one heart
　and breaks another
Leaves emptiness, despair
But then, the one
　that's left behind
Has great memories to share.

Kind people offer platitudes
Say, in time it will get better
They cannot know the lonely pain,
　the loss of laughs, the
　Thought you'd be here forever.

Yet, I know, you have not left,
You're just over the horizon,
　I can hear you
Your voice, your song,
　no you're not really gone
In memory, I'll always be near you.

HAPPY VALENTINE'S DAY

I wish I could be the first one to say
"Happy Valentine's Day", in your ear.

But, wishes and dreams
Don't always come true
Yet, I can't stop wishing you were here.

The touch of your hand
The sound of your voice
When you say "Hi"
How it thrills me.

My caroming heart beats ever so fast
No question, your love still fulfills me.

I only see you once in a while
But each meeting is priceless and precious;

And somehow I know that you love me, too
And you're gentle and kind.
You're so gracious.

So, I sit here and muse
And listen to the news
About the world and its many disasters;

And I still wish I could be the first one to say
Happy Valentine's Day, forever after.

I'm too old to believe the
Fairy tales that we read
Of happiness, love –
  and riding off into the sunset—.

   B u t –

Johnnie Mathis just sang,
"I Get Misty- Whenever You're Near"
And God knows that I dream
Of the day and the year
When I whisper, my dear,
Happy
Valentine's Day, in your ear.

FROM FRIEND TO FRIEND

(What About Me??)

Friend #2 talks to Friend #1:

To be born around Christmas
   is a curse and a blessing.
You were a 'treat' to your mother at best
She was so grateful you came
   healthy and early
So she could have the day
   before Christmas to rest.

Coming before Christmas
   was marvelous for her
No matter how she expressed it –
   But as birthdays go and come –
Yours was rolled into one
It was almost as though
   your folks had discussed it.

So Christmas is here, it's the 25th
And from here on –
   all gifts are a problem.
You can't have a party,
   no cake and no presents
So sorry, more problems,
   and no way to solve them.

What a heartbreak to learn
   that at each and every turn
On the 23rd of December –
   You were left out!
'Cause everyone else
   had birthdays at different times
And you, my friend, were ready to shout –
   "What about me??"

Brothers and sisters all got their due
And then, special gifts under the tree
But you got your presents
   combined at one time
And you'd holler silently,
   "What about me??"

Why is it they can get separate gifts
And you always – maybe –
   get one.
It isn't fair that you have to share
   with Christmas
Whenever it comes!!

Friend #1 to Friend #2:

Yeah, year after year it happens
And I get short-changed —
   here's the drift –
That there is –   only so much money
And I will get only one gift!!

IT JUST ISN'T FAIR!@!

      ^>^>^>^

Friend #2 to Friend #1:

You should change your natal day
To one in June or July
Maybe then, you'll get
   special treatment
And a cake and the trimmings –
   or maybe a pie
Which will make you feel
   childlike not vehement!

Maybe then, you'll get a ring
   and a nice gold chain
Or a tool chest for your car
   Or a sweater or maybe shoes,
   a jacket or a suit
Anything would be better – by far!!

      ^>^<^>^

Friend #1 to Friend #2:

Here's the caveat,
   my mind is made up!
Two birthdays a year I shall have!
   The first will be the 23rd of July;
The second, my usual, Dec 23rd –
   not too bad!

       ^<^>^<^

Now, Friend #2 to Friend #1:

   Listen, my friend:

The best part of the reason
   to celebrate
Is wrapped up
   in an exceptional package —

ITS YOU – ONLY YOU –

   And you've lived another year!!

So thank God – for your wonderful baggage!!

Did I Really Care Enough?

It was tattered and brown,
  well-used I would say
Falling apart from old age, anyway.

Looked for it on the bottom shelf
  in the kitchen
It wasn't there – I tried the pantry
Could find it nowhere.

Lost or stolen – I don't believe it
Wherever it is – I must retrieve it!!

The cover was off and it was held by
  a limp rubber band
There were some pages missing –
  but all-in-all –
   it was a grand piece of work –
I don't know how old.
It was so precious – couldn't be bought or sold –
And I could not find it!!

In the margins were love notes of instructions
  as to how
To cut, slither or break-up or substitute – Wow!!

Some pages were folded back
  to make things easier to find
And some had a grease spot or two,
  or some color, red or lime.

There were newspaper clippings
  to give it some class.
There were short or long explanations
  of experiences long past.

I sat down on the floor in front of the cabinet –
Looked meticulously through the books,
  some old and some new.

Then, my husband tramped into the kitchen—
   looked down on me and asked,
"What are you about to do?"
I said, "I'm looking for an old, old book,
  and I need it right now!"
"Oh, really?" He began to say,
"There was an old piece of junk
   held together by an even older rubber band –
   and – the pages kept falling out,
   whenever my hand would touch it.
 Got on my nerves, so I threw it away!!!"

I gasped, and finally said, "It was an old,
  cherished relic of mine – given to my mom
  by my grandmother at one time.
Mom shared it with me when she taught me
  to cook.
  It was full of tradition and history —
      It was Her COOKBOOK!!
I loved to page through.
It must have been something
  when it was brand new!! —
The love notes, the poems, sayings and directions –
  were like traveling back in time.
It could help you create almost anything to perfection.

A pinch of this, a dash of that, a sprinkle –
   don't measure –
   just taste. A splash of love and then shove it
   into the oven –
   don't waste – anything!"

I said, "It was <u>not</u> just an old-worn-out
   good-for-nothing book!
HOW COULD YOU?   And then I stood up.

He said, "I didn't know" – and then silence –
   (a very dramatic touch.)
Of course, I am sure he was thinking –
"If it meant so much to her why didn't she
   take better care of it – why didn't she share it –
   cover it with silk and roses,
   put it on a shelf in a glass case and close it –
   have a special place to expose it? N o w – ".

As I looked at him with sheer disgust —
   then called on the Lord —
I could only think of the should's and could's
   and why's.
His silence I hoped was kindness or remorse –
   Was he tongue-tied?

I sat back down on the floor and cried ——!!
   Dear Lord, please give me strength!!

DAWNING

As I gaze out of my dining room window
I see the silver mist cast upon the
  dogwood tree,
Clothed in its holiday orange-red,
  winking back at me.

The holly bush announces fall's
  grand entrance
And I can see at a glance, it's going to be
A wonderful day.

I marvel at the dawn, the rising
  of the sun in the East
The glory of it all.

Oh, yes, I'm ready for this adventure,
  the stroll around the park.
Not quite spelled out, not in the least.
An introduction, a phone call,
  a meeting planned, what a lark!

Ah, a knock on the door,
  a feast of wonders, he is really here.
Hopefully, this is the dawning,
  the beginning not the end
Of a new and wonderful friendship!

P.S.: I LOVE YOU

I'm looking at the grandeur
   Of the blue sky'
Watching God paint
   and re-paint the trees.

Though alone, I'm certainly not lonely
He is speaking to me
   And my heart is pleased.

Knowing soon,
   the darkness will conceal it –
This beautiful painting that I see.

It's really what we call a 'sneak preview'
   And I believe He painted it just for me.

Yet, I know, too,
   this beauty shown, won't cease -
   because the moon will shine.
   and stars will sparkle brightly –

And my once troubled heart
   will be at ease.

Love is such a strange and 'heady' feeling
Only lovers can describe its charms
God shares His love and Masterfully
   soothes our feelings
   and we are blessed
   while wrapped within His arms.

Sitting in the quiet of the evening
   wishing you, my lover were here –

This has always been our favorite place
  I miss your voice, your touch, your face

Is that a gardenia peeking through
   the moonlight?
Its wonderful aroma fills this space.

It's been so long since you've been
    home
(I know I'm rambling in this letter).

I pray that our world will soon be at peace.
   and He will send you, my heart, my love,
     here

  to me,
    tonight,
      tomorrow,

  or please,

  Dear God,

     this year.

IV.

Thoughts and Dreams

THIS REALLY HAPPENED – OR WAS I DREAMING???

I woke up this morning
  with a smile on my face
I first thanked my God
  for his limitless Grace!

I turned on my side
  as the phone rang quite loudly
And heard a small voice that said
  "Mom!" oh so proudly!

"I just thought I'd call you
  before going to school –.
I know it's so early
  but I didn't break any rules.

Dad is out in the garage
  just waiting for me,
But, I had to say
  I love you, so much, can't you see?"

"Tommy next door says
  grow up and don't cry;
But why did you leave me
  without saying goodbye?"

"Mommy, it's so lonely,
　especially at night.
Daddy and I get along we don't fight.
　But,
I don't have you to listen and sing to
　and
Nobody like you to bring my school papers
　and drawings to.
Nobody to laugh with
　when I make funny faces
Nobody to catch ball and to go fun places."
　　(sigh)
"Daddy says you're in heaven
　and will always be there -
But, Mommy, I need you
　in heaven down here!"

"I promise to be good
　and mind Daddy, he's tired - .
He works so hard and so much –
　maybe he'll get fired!

Just say you love me
　like you always do and
I won't call again,
　unless Daddy tells me to."

I said to this small voice,
　"I love you so much
And I'll always be near you,
　so close you can touch!"

"Bye Mommy; Oh, Mommy, I love you!"

Click went the phone.
(Did this really happen?)

I believe this child thought he was
   dialing Heaven,
And the number turned out
   to be mine. (I have no Children.)

MY DREAMS –

   DREAM #1 –

I found myself in a strange large
Capsule, deep red in color, seeming to be
made out of suede with
about six different passengers –
It opened up like a flower.
Everyone seemed to have a particular
position/job to do. We talked about
how we got here in the middle of the
ocean – and someone said that the
helicopter dropped us down during the
night so that no one would know
where our expedition was.

It seemed we were all scientists –
and I was the only African-American
in the bunch – there did seem to be
other nationalities there. Three.
It seemed after a time three were
sitting at a round table mapping out
something.
I was called by another to see
what I could do about
a strange scorpion-like spider–.
there were two of them that were
of a very dangerous species.

Apparently, I was in my bare feet
and I walked over to them –.
Very quickly one had spun its web
around my ankle. I swooped it up
and carried it kite-like to the back
of a chair and wrapped the spider
web around the back of the chair,
leaving the bug kite-flying there.
Then, I did the same thing with
the other spider. When I walked
back to the table they asked what
I had done and I told them the
method used. They seemed to be
impressed and apparently that was
my forte – as a scientist, to know
what and how to do things with bugs.

It seemed a little later on,
(because everyone had changed
clothes and was in a uniform- like
outfit –dresses, sleeveless and long,
flowing, of pastel colors, and
tight pants for the men), that we
were to make a pact with each
other that we would give
our lives for each other.–
This pact was made by each person
hugging the other one.

Everyone was very serious.
I remember hugging one of
the women who was rather strange
looking and, making a pact with her
gave me an eerie feeling. I thought
to myself do I really want to do this?

I wonder if there is more to this
than meets the eye.

I then, woke-up. (Relieved-Ha!)

DREAM #2

In my next dream –
One of my friends had given me,
and my mother was with me,
a plane equipped with engine,
movable wings and the like,
about two feet long.(wingspan).

I felt it was a nice gift
but I wasn't too sure just what
to do with it.
Apparently we couldn't fly it
outside, so we had to fly it
in the house.

My mother,
who was always game
for something like this, wound it up
or did whatever needed to be done
to make it fly.

We threw it up into
the ceiling just to see what it would do.

Believe it or not, it flew,
and then crash-landed, streaking oil
and rust colored stuff on the rug.

The lights went out so it apparently
did something to the electricity and
when it came back on, my mother
was wiping up what I thought was
the oil streak from the plane,
but she said she was getting up
some flower leaves that she had
stepped on while watching
the plane, and they had been
crushed in the rug.

I threw it up
and outward this time.
It flew around while we watched,
and then silence.
We looked for the plane, knowing
it had landed again, somewhere
in the house which seemed
to have very high ceilings.
And lo and behold, it was stuck
up in the ceiling.

We wondered how we
could get it down – I woke up.

Hang in there –
    Things come in threes:
        Another Dream: #3.

I remember going out to dinner
with my 'Best and Only', (B & O),
and having parked my car
in the front- right in front –
of the restaurant.
There were signs there
but I paid no attention –
since I was early and
he had not yet arrived.

After a wonderful evening,
we left the restaurant
and my car was not there.
It was dark and I couldn't
believe my car was not parked
where I left it.

He seemed to think I couldn't
remember where I had parked
the car and drove off and left me –
standing there.

I said I would never forgive him
for that
and I was A N G R Y.

I found out from the
parking-caddy that my car
had been towed to the garage
which was right next door
and all I had to do was go get it;
there would be no charge. Phew!

Strangely enough, I had had
some parts of this dream before –
where my car
was not to be found,
but had been parked in an
underground, dark, spooky garage
nearby.
I was still STEAMING –
but went home to bed-— when
the phone rang –
Awakened me – from my dream –
and guess who it was –
'my used-to-be' B and O.

When I told him
how glad I was that he had
awakened me,
and told him how angry I was
with him in my dream, he said,

"Now I have to defend myself,
even in your dreams".

We both got a big kick out of that!

SUPERSTITIONS – @!!# @##!!

Just what my papa said!

Papa says –: Watch where you walk and
             Don't walk under a ladder;
It could be hard on your health
  and ruin your bladder.

I don't know, I just did it,
  But that's what my Papa says.

Papa says–: When a dog is howlin'
  and there's no moonlight in the sky,
  No clouds flying and no star shining;
Someone is about to die.

I don't know, I ain't seen it,
But that's what my Papa says.

Papa says –: When you break a mirror–
   seven years of bad luck
And if you're left-handed.
   you owe the devil –
     seven years of catching the buck.

I don't know, he's left-handed
But that's what my Papa says.

Papa says-: When your palm is itchin'
      If you hold something cold
in your hand
If it's your left-hand –you'll kiss a fool;
      If it's your right-
you'll get some money –
Get enough money for a one night's stand.

I don't know, I ain't itchin'
But, that's what my papa says.

Papa says: If you open up your
  umbrella inside
It'll bring you bad luck,
  and give you blisters on your thighs.

And when the sun is shining,
  and the rain is coming down
  The devil's beating his wife – I say –
    What a clown!

I don't know – I ain't seen him
But, that's what my papa says.

Papa says: If you see a woman
  in a fiery red dress
  with a silk hat and feather cocked on her head
    She's up to no good, and good for nothin'
    But, he bets she sure is good in bed.

I don't know. I won't touch that
But, that's what my papa says.

Papa says: If you sweep
  all your dirt out the door
  instead of dust-pannin' it off the floor
  You sweep all your luck away
  'Cause that's what the dustpan is for – he say.

      And when you're sweepin'
      Don't touch him with the broom
      'Cause he'll go straight to jail –
      And won't come back soon.

I don't know – I ain't never touched him
But, that's what my papa says.

Papa says: When a black cat crosses your path –
      Bad luck! Bad luck!
      I'm runnin' fast!
      Cats are scary, and my luck won't last!
      I can see it comin' – what am I gonna do?
      All this gloom and doom, I know it's true!
      'Cause that's what my papa says!

Papa says: When you want to get married
      You gotta jump the broom.
      If your feet touch the handle
      Then. You ain't no bride and groom.
      You got no business marryin'
      It's much too soon.

I don't know – I ain't got a boyfriend
But, that's what my papa says.

Mama stuck her head in the door
And said to papa: "What you tell her that for?"

She said: "Men are bad luck!" Hands on her hips
     Her head shakin' and pursin' her lips
     "Mark my words child, kill me dead!
     Men's a heap of trouble, child –
     Don't care what your papa said!!"

PLEASE SAY YES

Swing your hips, girl, round and round
Lift your arms and turn around
Cast your eyes across the room
See your fella with this broom?

Raise your eyes up to the sky –
Your dark hands lifting way up high –

It's a circle that you make-
All those gifts are yours to take
Blanket, basket, ribbon too,
   bucket, thimble, just for you.

Swing your hips, girl – twirl around
Lift your feet up off the ground!

It's your wedding night – you see –
Special time for you and me!

I feel that fire in your breast
Not 'til dawn you get some rest.

Folks, hold that sweep broom
  way up high
We gone jump it by and by.

Swing your hips, girl –
  round and round!
Hear my hands clap –
  my heart pound?

Massa came and Massa left
He don't know what we know best
Love ain't somethin' – you can buy
Can't make pretend – Love don't lie.

By tomorrow you'll be my wife –
He may sep'rate us –
  but we're for life!!

And I promise you my girl
Someday our chillen –
  have a new world.

No more pickin' cotton,
  no more whips!
No more brands, cut hands, split lips.
Dance for me, girl – move your hips.

Please my pretty, be my wife
And I'll love you all my life.

OUR PALMS

Our palms are an intricate part of us,
feather-like and fan-shaped
Beautiful with five extensions
Sensitive with few pretensions
You get what you see.

We use our palms to wave at a group,
   to say this is the end, to salute
To dap and to clap, to extend friendship,
   to recognize kinship
To fortune-tell our lives,
   count husbands or wives
To follow a roadmap,
   to shade our eyes or take a nap
To buckle and button,
   to pull up or push down.

To say stay or come,
   to measure when done
To slap hard or tap light,
   to say well-done or start a fight
Without a palm there is no taxi,
   no directions from the back seat
No shaking, no waking,
   no baking, no taking.

Our palms may be soft and/or sensuous,
   have corns or be rough;
Be dainty or strong, limp, moist or tough –
   are for clasping or blowing,
Praying, catching or throwing!

We receive the 'bread of life'
   in our palms in supplication
We blow a kiss from our palm
   with love and appreciation.
Like so many other things,
   we take our palms for granted.
They tell our life's story,
   from birth 'til we're planted —

Please open your palms
   in a way that's inviting
Bless each other warmly
   in a way that just might be
The sweetest words
      you've ever heard,

THE PAT ON THE BACK!

THE PAT ON THE BACK!.

BELIEVE ME, IT'S NICE TO BE HOME

After I've traveled to exotic places;
eaten strange foods
and looked in strange faces,
Marveled at sunsets
from Hamburg to the Casbah (in Casablanca)
 to Rome –
It's so nice to be home.

Moved around on buses,
in taxis and trains,
pushcarts and man-pulled sleds,
ships and on planes;
slept during their days
and rambled at nights;
Missed reservations, tickets and flights –

Gargled in coke and wrapped
my sore toes;
sponged- bathed in cold water
where anything goes;
given up my passport
and lost half my clothes – Yes,
It's nice to be home.

Climbed the Tower of Pisa's
steep narrow steps
and watched flamingoes march in pairs;
Saw Queen Mary's guillotine
and sat in Queen Liz's chair;

In Madrid, dined on six courses—
about midnight— fit for a king;
gulped cool water in the desert—
right from a spring;

Was given a bull's ear from the Matador
   we met,
And cheered for the bull who was saved;
Even yet, I dream of the pageantry,
Excitement and fear –
For both bullfighter and animal
Whose lives were so dear.

Eaten the best steaks and fries
From the top of the Eiffel Tower;
Compared the grandiose castles of
Kings and Queens with great power.

Was escorted by a Monsignor,
Had an audience with the Pope;
Enjoyed a gondola ride on the Volga
When of all things – my sandal strap broke.

Drank wine from the vineyards
And ate olives from the groves
Rode camels that stank
And counted friendly apes toes.

Watched big rats in the marketplaces
   after the fun;
Caught two kids stealing my purse
   and put them on the run —
There is NO place like home.

Moved by seeing the Favellas
  Teeter-tottering up in the hills
And watched the children slide
  down from the top on straw mats –
  with very few spills.
Threw coins in the blue-green ocean
  To the beautiful youngsters
  Diving not for thrills;

Fought the heat and the smell of sweat
  In the tiny mahogany mills;

Slept on short beds
  with even shorter quilts,
Saw a tribe so tall
  thought they were on stilts.
was pinched by some fella,
  as I walked out of the store
Was asked for autographs
And bought gargoyles and more — —.

Listened to bagpipes
  and laughed at plaid kilts;
checked out the parade guards
and how beautifully they were built.
  How humbling it is to be home.

Visited cathedrals
  and gazed at mountains in awe.
Watched women on a veranda,
  weaving pretty baskets of straw.
Flew over waterfalls, filmed glaciers,
  Sipped coffee;

Drank watermelon juice, bought stale
   chewing gum, and unwrapped toffee.
Tasted warm beer, and sang lusty French songs,
Heard bells, Allahs, chimes, drums and gongs.
   It's nice, oh, it's nice to be home.

Shopped in marketplaces
and haggled with the best of them;
Fought flies, and mosquitoes,
   at night with the rest of them;
Ate conch, raw fish, eel and poi
   with hot mustard,
Ate goat and horsemeat, snake, coconuts
   and custard.

Had stomach aches, back aches,
   head aches and sore feet;
Yet, enjoyed every minute away –
   Each time was a traveling treat!
Got cranky, and sweaty, and dirty – to boot;
Came home laden with parcels and packages –
   and an elephant or two.

Got seasick, carsick and homesick away;
Got better and tougher and more
   inquisitive each day.

Bought paintings and crystal, gold,
   silver and white linen;
Watched children and women work in
   human factories, along with the men.
Felt sadness, yet happiness when
   actually touched by them.
   (We are all part of the human race).

I'm home now, with hot water, and
   real queen-sized sheets;
And seldom have to run for my life
   crossing the streets??

Can drive down the highway and
   know where I'm going? Can go to
   the movies and
   understand what's showing?
Can order Pizza delivered,
   have soft toilet paper, crisp bacon;
Can really appreciate things
   for granted, I've taken.

Wouldn't trade my experiences for
   anything in the world,
For each time I return,
   I'm a much wiser girl.

Home to the waiting arms
   of someone I love.
Home with many thanks
   to my Creator above!

As soon as I've rested, saved money,
   made plans, I'll be ready to go again
   to see more strange lands!

(HAS IT DAWNED ON YOU YET?)

I'LL SAY IT AGAIN,
   HOPE YOU DO GET
      THE MESSAGE!

Be happy with what you have
   And do count your blessings!!

BELIEVE ME,
  IT'S NICE TO BE HOME!

V.

Good Grief!
Life is Great!!

THIS BUSH IS MINE!!

You're watching me
  And I'm watching you
    As I flitter and flutter
    The way I'm supposed to.

I'm a little Butterfly,
  I'm powerful and quiet;
I love to sip from these flowers,
They're all on my diet.

I'm methodical and particular
  And I will not be rushed.
It upsets me when another Butterfly
  Comes poking 'round my bush.

I'll fight to the end
  To keep my property
For my wife and my little ones –
  My whole family.

Sometimes there are so many
  good things to eat,
That I stuff myself –
  these flowers are all such great treats!

But don't think 'cause I'm pleasant
  And smiling all the time
That I'm not possessive –
  I want to keep what is mine!

  I flutter and flitter
   and dive bomb sometimes,
from one flower to another
   in silent syncopated lines.

My wife and I fly in formation –
  watch us, we're beautiful
And we'll take the kids –
  teaching them what is dutiful.

Oh, yes, you like our colors,
  my color is basically yellow.
My wife is orange and black –.
I'm a jolly good fellow!

I appreciate your kindness,
  Your 'ooh-ing' and 'ah-ing'
So long as you recognize that –

This Bush is Mine!! —

I'll see you around.

VELMA'S PLACE

Way down in Birmingham, AL
   located in Ensley space
We went to a record emporium
   we'll call it Velma's Place.

The door was well –barricaded
   it was heavily shuttered and barred
Someone peeked out of a little slit –
   and pulled the door ajar.

Again, we rang the bell and waited-
   and someone opened the door.
We asked for the record lady
   and found she was on the third floor.

The building was dark
   and the door locked behind us –
It went through my mind –
   that no one could find us.
We quietly walked through
   a wide-open space
And were ushered up two flights
   of this fascinating place.

The first stairs were wide,
   both shallow and deep,
So, as you climbed upward,
   you minced, and shuffled, or
Did something more like a creep.

The second stairs went both
   downward and up
In a very dark hallway,
   and were very steep.

We climbed upward slowly,
   trying hard to see,
And, whew, we could hear
   the old steps creak.
My eyes widened,
   I'd never seen so much stuff,
     So much junk.
I mean, such a decidedly
   disorganized conglomerate with
So many different pieces of things –
And parts of it or whatever it – was.
Like a buffet table
   with bits and pieces
   of everything on it.

And then, I saw VELMA.

She was round all over
   with arms like a wrestler
And sensitive hands
   but you wouldn't want to test her.
Her skirt went down to her ankles
Her bare feet were stuffed in scuffs
Her smile was warm
   she had a pleasant voice.
Yet, her manner was somewhat rough.

She swayed languidly
   when she walked about
A silk rag wrapped around her head.
She had a worldly way about her
   when she laughed –
And you wondered
   if she'd just gotten out of bed.

I sat on a crooked bar stool
   and kept sliding off the seat.
It was next to a rickety old glass case
That housed old accordions,
   keyboards and cleats,
A grimy old ashtray
   and a very large vase.

There was an old smell,
   a cold smell, a mold smell
      That hung
Like the aftermath of a circus
Where they cleaned up camel dung.

There were old chairs,
   old portfolios, old stools
      And plaques –
Old boxes, old tapes,
   old doors and candle wax.
There were old curtains,
   old couches, old fans
      And old mikes –
Old turnstiles,
   old phonographs and records
      Of all types.

There were old walls,
   old stalls, and old halls –
      Dust everywhere –
That clung, twirled and crawled,
   and hung in the air.

There were old tweeters,
   old speakers, old TV's,
      And jackets –
Old shelves and old lampshades,
   and cassettes in old packets.

There were old air ducts,
   old archways, old rooms
      And old tables.
Old bars and old pipes.
   Carpenters horses
      From old stables.
Old mules and old ladders,
   and old sheet music with stars;
Old violins, old tools
   and a seat from an old car.

There were old 45's,
   12 inch records, old albums
      And colored paper –
Old mannequins, old bulbs,
   old brooms, and an old elevator.

Old music, good music, fast music,
   and true blues.
I'll tell you those moments
   called for my dancing shoes.

There were high dirty ceilings,
   windows broken,
Rafters splitting,
   stove and lady smoking.

Cracks in the floorboards,
   paint peeling, old atmosphere
   with a very warm feeling.

Line drawings on the walls of
   Great bodies, lithe and tall.–
Dancing. with abandon –
   and full feeling
Bodies twirling, faces reeling!!

Silhouettes of lovers –
   so enchanting while romancing;
Lone expressive faces in pictures
      On the walls
And great portraits of black musicians.
Believe me, that's not all!

The heart of Velma is all over the place
Like the paper and wrappers
   and discarded plates.
Old music, sweet music,
   hot music, sad blues
This rhythm. Just tappin'
   goes down to my shoes!

Her voice speaks with pleasure
She loves doing what she does
And the age of the place
   and it's history
Make no impression on her –
   because

Velma's place is something else –
For young music and old tunes,
   If you'd rather.
The place takes you back
   in your memory bank
As you hear one song
   played after the other.

This place is a dream!
You'll have the time of your life.
It's a happening –
   that'll help you forget
      Sadness and strife.

Velma will tape any record
   for you, jazz, rock and roll
Any song or part of it,
   from the newest to the old.

When you get home
   and you play back your tape
You'll find half the songs aren't on it;
So you have to return to this –
   fascinating place-
So she'll do it right this time –
   Doggone it!!

That's Velma's Place!!

AT THE POLLS

Sitting pretty in my pink –
　waiting for the folks to come
Nothing much to do, I think –
They trickle in – One by One.

The place is set up – fixed just right
Signs and posters all in sight.
We'll be here until tonight
Watching them come, One by One.

Brought our food,
　drinks and our snacks
Some in tote bags or back-packs
Counting voters – real low score,
One an hour, sometimes more –
One by One.

At each hour we report
Very few but we're good sports
Read our papers and our books
One by One.

Set our flag up and our tables
Been here since the crack of dawn
We're so cold now,
  yet we're able to thaw out –
  out in the sun.

Waiting, waiting, oh, so patiently
Want to go and holler loud
Come to vote, come to our station.

Y'all come please, and bring a crowd –
  One by One!

All of a sudden, when 6:50 pm rolls around –
Here you come – Two by Two.

Be careful what you ask for —
It just might come true!!

TOENAIL POISONING

I MUST TELL YOU GOOD FOLKS
  WHAT HAPPENED TODAY –
Needless to mention,
  it got me to pray.

I injured my great toe
  in a left-handed way
And for a couple of weeks, now,
  I've noticed a decay.

Well, I mentioned it at work
  and my co-workers did cluck
They couldn't imagine me,
  a person with pluck
Letting my great toe be
  my whole conversation.
The way it was hurting,
  I'd have told the whole nation.

So, with urging from friends
  I decided to go
To the Emergency Room,
  to see about my toe.

A dear friend who works there,
  greeted me at the door
Made arrangements for me,
  and before I could utter a word

A nurse asked me to show –
  her the bane of my existence –
To wit – my big toe.

Well, she uttered a gasp,
  and then enunciated slowly
"My dear, I'm afraid your big toenail
  must go!"

Wow! Not one to relinquish
  My body parts so easily
I wailed very loudly,
  the answer is "NO"!

So, she made an appointment
  in an hour for a surgeon
Ignored my complaints –
  that MY nail they were splurging.

I thought surely the surgeon would say.
  "We're much too busy –
To take the time to remove
  a big toenail from a dizzy woman
  who wants to keep the thing anyway –" .

Instead. Two surgeons said,
  "We must remove this thing today!"

They checked blood work and vitals,
  and found I was healthy
Both said, "To Minor Surgery
  immediately we'll go!"

I said, "Hold your horses,
  you need my permission!"
The head surgeon said,
  "Are you giving us a hard time?
  Let's go!"

In shock – and reluctantly,
  I was whisked down the hall
With two doctors and two students –
  barking orders –
    From the large to the small.

We entered a darkened room
  and I was placed in a barber chair
And on came a bright light on my foot –
  and with laissez faire –
The Doc said "I'll tell you everything
  that we do –
And by the way,
  you won't be wearing
  anything like a shoe for a while." –
Believe it or not he said it with a smile.

He said, "We're going to deaden
  your toe right away –
And you won't feel a thing
  for the rest of the day.

I'd advise you to close your eyes
  and listen to what I say.
Do you have any questions?"
  I said, "No, I'll just pray."

They brought out a needle,
  the longest I'd ever seen
They proceeded to inject anesthesia,
  the pain was quite keen
    for a while.

I closed my eyes,
  knowing I couldn't stand to look –
But the chair was uncomfortable –
  so I laid back
With a crook – in my neck.

The Doc asked,
"Do you feel anything?" I said, "No" –
So, with great pulling, wrenching,
  grinding and twisting –

Another wrench and a tear –
  I sat mute in my chair
A high stream of blood –
  flew up in the air – @@ –
They removed my big toe(nail).

The blood gushed out everywhere,
  and covered the floor
    (too much information –Ha)
The students got panicky,
  one headed for the door.

The doctor said,
  "Compression! Much harder
  and do it quick!"
As I looked up and saw all this –
  "I think I'll be sick!"

The surgeon said, "You'll be fine;
Right now, your blood won't coagulate –
Have you taken any aspirin
  or Bufferin of late?
I said, "I really don't think so,
  I've taken some Motrin."
In unison they said,
  "That's the reason,
  it makes your blood thin."
I said, "Oh!"

They made with light chatter
  as the Doc squeezed my toe
And for about fifteen minutes
  he wouldn't let go!

He was covered with blood –
  it was mine –
  but – he – looked pale.
I thought – next is a transfusion –
  God, humans are so frail.

Then the doctor said quite loudly
  (as if I were deaf)
"We've stopped the major flow –
And in a few minutes, after dressing it,
  you can go."

He said, "Three or four days
  it will bother you,
And here's what you do –soak it,
  Bacitracin it, bandage it too –
But don't wear, do you understand,
  don't wear a closed shoe!"
  (still talking like I'm stone deaf-
  or don't speak English).

I said, "I'm here by myself,
  can I drive my car home?"
He said very loudly,
"You didn't tell me you came here alone!"
     (He hesitated for the first time)

"But, if you must drive,
  be very careful and go slow,
'Cause your foot is quite dead –
  not to mention your toe."

The Doc looked me
  'dead in the eye' and said,
  "Have no fear –
You'll have a new toenail
  in just about a year". (Smiling clearly).

"When you get home –
  take this medicine – off your feet –
And in the bed, you'll sleep tonight.–
  It will be 24 hours before
All feeling will return –
  instead, you'll have pain
  and discomfort
And bleeding, just a mite."

He finished the packing
   and wrapping and said,
"What a beautiful sight!"

Well, needless to say, I'm at home
and in pain –
Hope I never have to go
   through this ordeal again
And I thank God for nine toenails,
   when I used to have ten!

The Good Lord watched over me,
   my hand in His the whole time –
I repeat – I'm so grateful –
   at least I have nine – Toenails!!!

THE SURVIVOR

It always seems so strange to see
Just one leaf hanging from a tree.
It seems to happen in one season –
Winter. There must be a reason.

Here this leaf hangs, by itself,
  all – Alone.
It's the last child left at home.

Would you call it a wallflower? Ha!
Only it's standing tall, not on a wall.
Perhaps lonely, but that's all –
Withstanding wind, snow and
  much rainfall
Sunshine, frost and a small squall.

It had family, father, mother
Aunts, and uncles, sisters and brothers –
Tell me – where have they all gone?

Leaving this leaf, tenacious, strong – .
It knows what survival means –
As it's tossed and turned –
  it leans
  Against the wind and holds the snow –
Where'd all the other family go???

Think of life in this same way
There are those who always stay –
Those who really stick it out
And the ones who do drop out
Or pass away – or as leaves do.
Don't hold on – but toss and sway
Until the loosened grips give way.

In life we hang too, 'til the end
No matter how life lifts or bends.

I think that I shall never see
A leaf so lonely on a tree –
(It smacks of Kilmer),
   hanging free
This leaf is haunting, taunting me.

Holder, mender, laugher, thriver,
Loner, groaner, braver, enabler,
  stabilizer
And with this a 'Strong Survivor!!

It always seems so strange to see
Just one leaf hanging from a tree!
It's wonderful to be
        A Survivor!!

The Mysterious Old Gentleman

There is an old man who walks every day
And I've noticed him walking
  when I'm on my way — home.

He's tall, and gaunt,
 and about 80-years old
But walking quite upright,
  not stooped, looking bold.

His clothes are slightly old-fashioned
Pants high at the ankle
His jaunty hat cocked over his eye
His jacket, not a wrinkle.

I wonder what his story is
He looks so neat and clean
And my imagination romps – ,
To him, – what does life mean?

I ask myself these questions:

Was he a plumber, soldier or preacher
His glory was what kind?
Perhaps, a miner, blacksmith or teacher
I keep mulling these over in my mind.

I'll bet once he was a sailor –
  standing wide-legged on a deck
Belching out loud orders –
  and just giving his people heck.
      A Sailor he was.

Or maybe he was a tailor,
   meticulous and trim
And all the fine ladies and gentlemen
Would bring their business to him –
   to be suited and dressed
   In the most gorgeous material
And to be gowned, tuxed and modeled –
   to look starlike and ethereal.
         A Tailor, he was.

Or, maybe he was a hat-maker,
   a 'hatter' would be what they'd call him
Who shaped, molded and finished
   men's hats –
Just the way that they told him.

Panamas and Stetsons and Fedoras galore,
   Grey chapeaux and black ones,
      top hats – in his store.

And just for the ladies, an ostrich or two
   Have given their best feathers –
      to create 'a beauty for you'.
And curled felts and flat straws
   and great silken turbans
For women in mansions
   and those in suburbans.
         A Hatter, he was.

Or, maybe he plowed acres,
   cotton or corn was his crop
And walked with his plow horse,
   up and down rows
   until he was ready to drop.
       A Farmer, he was.

Maybe he picked bananas in the heat,
   in Jamaica
And longed for a better way to survive
So he stowed away on a banana boat –
   lucky to reach Florida shores alive.
       A Banana picker, he was.

I bet he had a family,
   with three girls and four boys
And two wives in his 80-odd years
And he's living with one of his
   children right now
In a place that gives shelter,
and now and then tears.

He had two sisters
   and one brother as well,
And they've been apart
   for a very long spell.

But now, friends and family
   have passed – one way or another
And he's outlived his sisters
   and has only one brother.

So, this unknown gentleman
   walks every day
Up and down the roads in our area
And he stops once in a while
   and faces the sun
As he prays for a final scenario
   of friends and grandchildren
All gathered around,
   hearing the sounds of many,

Telling him how much they love him.
      A Family man, he was.

I know that he yearns
   for yesterday's warmth
Since these times are cold,
   and the great life's outgrown him
And the wonders of the world
   have taken their toll
While the Wise Spirit above
  Is showing him what –
      An Ancient Struggler, he is.

He remembers the days
   of toiling in the sun
And in the rain, while he's getting soaked;
   and of rushing to catch
   time on the run
As he gathers his loneliness
   around him, like a cloak.
      A Lonely man, he is.

He asks the Wise Spirit
   for a companion to walk with
So the two of them can reminisce;
And he finishes his prayer,
   giving thanks for his blessings –
I'll bet that's what his story is.

This gentle, sensitive, slow of gait,
   slow to hate,
Quick to love, sending thanks above,

Man alone walking home —

Grabs the crumbs of happiness
   where he can
'Cause he's part of the Wise Spirit's plan

And he and the Spirit walk hand-in-hand.

This way, you know, he cannot be —
   a Lonely Man.
      A Grateful Man, he is.

YOU BEAUTIFUL ROSE

I see you peeking
 out from your
 emerald leaf –
Oh, you
 extraordinary rose.

Many songs and sonnets
have been written about you
 and your beauty,
many poems and prose.

Let's not forget
your delicate fragrance
That lights up the entire garden,
 house, and lane.

No wonder the bees
 fight over you, and
Hummingbirds quickly do –
 the same.

Soon, your soft, silk-like petals
Will fall to the ground,
  not making a sound,
Covering it like a carpet

So that, we, life's children,
  girls and boys
Can continue to enjoy you –

You Beautiful Rose.

BECAUSE I'M GETTING OLD

Should I not love the smell of the ocean
  or the flow of my hair
  in the breeze, because I'm getting old?

Must I sit on the sidelines
  and not enjoy the beat,
  or act like I'm stone because I'm getting old?
  I must tap my feet!!

Should I act like the birds aren't singing
  their hearts out
And turn away from my pet
  when she wags to get out?

Should I give into pain in my back and my knees
  and no longer enjoy
  quietly sitting under the trees?

If I cry a little more, should I hide my tears –
  because I'm getting old?

There are a few more wrinkles
  and splotches and moles
And my memories are wonderful,
  but my memory has holes.
My thoughts sometimes wander,
  the same as a child's
  But, is that because I'm getting old?

Must I never have a lover or
  a warm body to feel?
Someone to bring flowers
  and make me feel real?
Must I cloud over the timeless
  twinkle in my eyes?
    Only because I'm getting old?

There's talk of retirement, —
  to what and to where?
My fears of being left behind,
  I can't even share,
But, my loving of living
  grows greater everyday —

It's SPLENDID because I'm getting older!!

TEACHER, TEACHER, TELL ME HOW

Teacher, Teacher, tell me how
  I can ever pass your tests?
When I study long and hard,
  you don't think I do my best.

Read assignments, graphs and polls,
  write your papers, do research-
Then, your notes in red are tricky,
  you use words not used in church.

Can it be that you don't like me –
  I always speak, remove my hat
I smile and nod along with your lectures
  maybe it's the nodding that
Gets your back up – makes you angry –
  Makes you think that I'm not smart!

Psychology is really heavy – yet –
  I'm good in music and art!

Teacher, Teacher, I'm really sorry –
  Hit you with that spit ball there
While you were 'splaining
  Maslow's Hierarchy –
    drawing pyramids in the air.

Teacher, Teacher,
  please don't fail me!! TEACHER??

PLEASE, PASS IT ON!

Has someone smiled at you, today?
Helped you on your lonely way
Said, "You go on. I can stay?"
    Pass it on.

Know that kindness, through the
 years
Will help wipe another's tears;
In God's book this deed appears.
    Please, pass it on.

Let your shoulders hold the weight
Once you've finished, you'll feel great
You have reaped the goodness sown,
   So, pass it on.

Talk is cheap, but words are great
Someone needs help, don't hesitate
There is always time to pray,
To your Maker, home or away–
    Please, pass your goodness on.

Spring is time for all to wake;
Summer is time for thoughts to bake;
Fall is when you correct mistakes,
Winter is when we all snuggle
  to keep warm-
 To weather the storms, to set alarms,
 And to say, "I'm sorry."
    Pass it on.

Give with hands open, arms spread wide
You have so much love inside;
Shed your meanness, share your pride–
    Pass it on.

Sometimes, love and hugs
    are all we have –
Smiles and laughter, giggles, too –
Music, warmth and jokes as well,
Share! It will all come back to you!!
      Believe me!
    So, please, pass it on!!

LE GENERALE

The boss said he wanted a portrait
  of a general who was leaving.
When can I do it, she asked,
  because time I don't have a lot?
He said, You can take it home to do,
  you're the only artist I've got
I could tie-up the rest of the folks together
  and you'd still come out on top."

"But, Mr B, why can't you see
  a thing like this takes time,
And I'm afraid my taskforce without me
  gets way out of line."

"Here are my instructions, Ms J,
    I'll hear no more about it –
And by the way, this is a surprise,
  the General can't know about it!"

"There must be photos taken
  in different poses and sizes;
One straight on, one side view
  and get a good one of his eyes.
  I'll get some family pictures
  that you can put around the sides —"

"And his house or the chapel
  or headquarters in the background,
  for which he has great pride.
Some bushes and trees, some flowers,
  to help make him look good;
And some of the soldiers he worked with,
  pull them out of the wood."

"I'm telling you that this is due
  this very time next week,
so my suggestion is stop complaining,
I know the situation is bleak."

So, she fretted but she started
  and she stayed up many nights;
  and during the day, she was so tired
  she and her staff had fights.

Then, the night before the unveiling
  which had quickly come around,
  she asked her friend to critique it,
  would she please just drive around.

Her friend had met the general,
  and knew just what to look for
  and to her surprise the painting could rise
  to any grand exhibit and more.
The general was not handsome
  and Ms J had much to do,
  but I was sure he would be happy
  with how he looked to me and you.

A work of art this painting,
  the general looked better in every way,
  he had fewer wrinkles, better color
  and he even had less gray.

The painting was presented
  and Le General went ape –
  his many exclamations of joy
  we should have put on tape.

I know this portrait is draping,
  yes smiling, over some large mantelpiece
  in Le General's home in the United States
  or perhaps Turkey, Japan or Greece.

Ms J will go down in history for doing
  the impossible, indeed, doing her best
and Mr B will never be forgiven
  for putting her to the test!

IT'S YOUR BIRTHDAY – OR IS IT MINE!!!

When it's your birthday
You're somebody special
Your every desire is attainable—.

Your walk is quite spritely
Your smile is much brighter
If you're over forty
Your youth seems regainable.

When it's your birthday
Your mind really wanders
It brings back sweet memories
  of long, long ago.

The mysteries your life held
The series of sadnesses
The reasons they happened –
You don't want to know.

But, yes! It's YOUR birthday –
You've made it another year
You've hung in there – Baby –
  through rain and through snow!

The sun now shines brightly
So we will all celebrate
'Cause you are the star of this –
  Broadway Show!

Hats Off!! To the lady
She's life's wondrous Aphrodite
Around her, surround her with love –
Watch her glow!

She loves all her birthdays,
   each one is so special
And she's such a good friend
We can't let her slow.

She'll always be young at heart
And never get older
Grabs life by the waistline
And she loves LIFE so!!

Yes!! We love her so!!

I SHOULD HAVE KNOWN –

I SHOULD HAVE KNOWN: THAT EVEN THOUGH
I CALLED THE BANK TO FIND OUT MY BALANCE
IN THE CHECKBOOK, AND WAS PROMISED THAT
THERE WERE OVER 300 DOLLARS READY
FOR RETRIEVAL, THAT THERE WAS ONLY $3.00
AND I WOULD BE PAYING PENALTY AFTER PENALTY.

I SHOULD HAVE KNOWN: THAT WHEN MY FRIEND
SAID HER CAT WOULD NOT COME NEAR ME
THAT AS SOON AS I SAT DOWN,
THE ANIMAL WOULD TRY TO JUMP IN MY LAP.

I SHOULD HAVE KNOWN:
THAT WHEN MY FATHER WARNED ME TO PUT GAS
IN HIS CAR FIRST, AND I FORGOT TO DO IT –
THAT THE GAS GAUGE WAS NOT WORKING PROPERLY
AND READ HALF FULL/EMPTY, THAT HE KNEW
WHAT HE WAS TALKING ABOUT,
WHILE I SAT ON THE SIDE OF THE ROAD.

I SHOULD HAVE KNOWN:
THAT- THAT LITTLE VOICE INSIDE ME
THAT KEPT SAYING YOU HAVE TO DO
SOMETHING AT CHURCH, KNEW THAT I WAS
SUPPOSED TO BE THE 'LAY READER' THAT MORNING –
WHILE I SAT PRIMLY IN THE PEW
AND FOLKS KEPT LOOKING AT ME STRANGELY.

I SHOULD HAVE KNOWN: THAT ON MY 15TH BIRTHDAY,
WHEN I WAS DANCING WITH THIS CUTE GUY,
AND EVERYONE ON THE DANCE FLOOR
SEEMED TO BE LOOKING AT ME,
IT WAS NOT BECAUSE I WAS SUCH A GREAT DANCER,
IT WAS BECAUSE MY SLIP HAD FALLEN DOWN
AROUND MY ANKLES, AND THEY WONDERED
HOW LONG I'D KEEP DANCING BEFORE
TRIPPING OVER IT.

I SHOULD HAVE KNOWN:
THAT THE LARGE PILE OF SHOES,
CLOTHES, BOOKS AND MAIL AT THE SIDE OF MY BED,
WOULD BE A BOOBY TRAP AND SEND ME
FOR A LOUD VISIT SCREAMING ACROSS THE ROOM
WITH A BROKEN TOE AMONG OTHER THINGS.

I SHOULD HAVE KNOWN: THAT THE TINY HOLE
IN MY STOCKING THAT I PLACED A SMALL DOLLOP
OF FINGERNAIL POLISH ON, WOULD GROW TO BE
A CAVERN ON MY LEG
EVEN BEFORE I GOT TO WORK.

I SHOULD HAVE KNOWN:
THAT THE TERRIBLE GROANING AND MOANING
IN MY GARAGE, LAST NIGHT, WAS MY CAR
WORKING THE SUSPENSION OR TRYING,
AND CALLING FOR HELP;
THE GAUGE DID SAY "CHECK SUSPENSION".
FOR WEEKS AND OF COURSE, I IGNORED IT.

*I SHOULD HAVE KNOWN:
THAT THE GRAPES ON THE OTHER SIDE
OF THE VINEYARD ARE NO SWEETER
THAN THE ONES YOU CAN PICK AND TASTE –
AND SO IS LIFE!!*

I SHOULD HAVE KNOWN – continued:

I should have known:
That there was a fly in the ointment when he said,
"I think the leak is coming from around the chimney.
Come on up on the roof with me and you can hand me
things." So, up the ladder I went, scrambled to the top,
and noticed he wasn't following. He yelled,
"Uh, I forgot something, I'll be right back."
I waited, and waited, watched the birds, and the clouds,
felt the breeze and the sun, changed my sitting position
(I'm on a steep roof, now) from side to side –
and constantly checked my watch, looked at the cars
rolling by – way out there on the road – one hour,
two hours. Started calling his name –
started calling him names!.

Yelled for help over and over again.
Started wondering if anyone would ever find me –
then, started wondering if anything had happened to him
– Heaven forbid -. He had removed the ladder,
– and driven off to get something (he said).
– By now, it was getting dark.
1. I should have remembered he was afraid of heights –
and too macho to tell me.
2. Perhaps he was punishing me for being
so comfortable on the roof
(watching the birds and bees, and stuff).
3. Where do you think he went?
What do you think he was doing??
How can you forget your wife is on the roof??

Finally he returned, put the ladder up, and fortunately for me, held it up, because by that time I was so stiff and s o o o mad — I could hardly move.   He thought the whole thing was hilarious. —
I should have known!!

I should have known: That when you visit someone in the country and you're walking along outside gazing at the stars, that you just might step into a hole, twist your ankle and never want to go to the country again.

I should have known: That when you get that giant ice cream cone, piled high with all of your favorite flavors, if you don't gingerly hold it with both hands and a napkin, it will go plop onto the ground leaving you with only the cone itself in your hand.

I should have known :
The very time you really believe your hairdresser will get you in and out (you have an appointment with her), in time for this heavy date, there'll be three other customers (no matter what the reason) before you — and you'll never make it on time.

I should have known: That when I asked
my landscaper to cut back the Crepe Myrtle tree
which was on the boundary line with my neighbor,
without consulting her, even though this is the way
you care for them each year, and I was paying for it,
that all Hades would break loose and the landscaper
went scurrying away from my property, never to return,
waiting until I returned home that evening to call me
and tell me about her actions,
and send his check in the mail.

I should have known: That when the mother asked me
to hold the baby for a few minutes,
that water would be coming out of it from both ends –
the baby was crying loudly, tears everywhere,
as soon as the mother left, and the baby's bottom
was soaking wet.

I should have known: That the large aluminum pan
in which I put the peach cobbler, was not strong enough
to hold it, and the pan would bend, practically fold up,
as I attempted to remove the cobbler from the oven.
What a mess!!

I should have known: That the six students
taken to another quiet classroom to take a makeup test,
and instructed not to cheat, (on their honor),
would check out each other's answers, not cheating,
just checking each other out.

I should have known: That when I called in sick
and I really was, but had to go to the drug store
to get some Kaopectate, that who would I run into —
but the principal.

I know by now:
That the grass is not greener on the other side,
that the husbands, wives and significant lovers
are no nicer to their 'significants' than
Mine — .
That every moment of life gets sweeter
as the years go by!

    LET'S KEEP ON SMILING
AND COUNT OUR MANY BLESSINGS!!

HOW DO WE DO IT?

How do we do it? –
Stay quietly up above the clouds?

What makes us so special –
That we have no doubts
About moving and flying
Higher and Faster?

The excitement we feel
  when we hear
The words "Blast-Off"!!

What makes us so special
That Fear is an energizer?

We face more and more danger
And don't seem the wiser.

Ah, yes how do we do it??

HELP!!!

ZZZZzzzzzzzZZZZZZZING
Ooh!!! What was that thing?

That must be a Bumble Bee.
It's moving so fast –
I really can't see!

Wow! Here it comes again
I don't know when –
 zzzzzZZZZZZING!
I've ever seen anything like it!

Here I am in my rose garden
Trying to cut one rose for my vase –
It's heading for my nose – Whew!
It just flew past my face – !

This is a disgrace –
This zzZZZZZing winging thing!

Ooh! There are two of them
Swooping and diving,
 faster than the wind!
I thought I was on MY property!
But I was mistaken,
these creatures aren't faking!
Apparently, this rose garden
 does not belong to me!

Oh, Goodness. HELP! –
I see Two Hummingbirds –
  and they mean business!!

I'm outa here!

ISBN 141207413-4